Washington, D.C.
Trivia Fact Book

WASHINGTON, D.C. TRIVIA FACT BOOK

FRANK J. FINAMORE

Gramercy Books
• New York •

This 2001 edition is published by Gramercy Books™,
an imprint of Random House Value Publishing, Inc.,
280 Park Avenue,
New York, NY 10017

Gramercy Books™ and colophon are trademarks of
Random House Value Publishing, Inc.

Random House
New York • Toronto • London • Sydney • Auckland

Printed and bound in the United States of America

Library of Congress Cataloging-in-Publication Data

Finamore, Frank J.
Washington, D.C. trivia fact book / Frank J. Finamore.
p. cm.
ISBN 0-517-21859-3
1. Washington (D.C.)—Miscellanea. 2. Washington (D.C.)—History—Miscellanea.
3. United States—Politics and government—Miscellanea. I. Title.

F194.6 .F56 2001
975.3—dc21
2001046016

8 7 6 5 4 3 2 1

CONTENTS

The White House

In 1791, Pierre Charles L'Enfant, an artist and engineer, worked closely with George Washington to prepare a city plan for Washington, D.C., which set aside eighty-two acres for a "President's Park."

✤   ✤   ✤

L'Enfant's "President's Palace"—as the White House was called in the original design—was about four times the size of the present White House. He envisioned a vast palace for the President. James Hoban, the architect in charge of the final approved design, substantially reduced the house's size.

✤   ✤   ✤

George Washington dismissed French engineer and architect L'Enfant for insubordination, and the design of the White House and Capitol was determined by separate architectural competitions in 1792. James Hoban, an Irish-born and trained architect then living in Charleston, South Carolina, won the design competition for the White House. Born in Kilkenny, Ireland around 1758, Hoban immigrated to the United States and worked as an architect and builder in Philadelphia and Charleston from 1785 until he moved to the Washington in 1792. He spent the rest of his life in there and became a prominent figure in construction and served

as a member of the City Council from 1802–1831. He died in Washington City in 1831.

＊　　＊　　＊

The construction of the White House began in 1792. It was first occupied by President John Adams in 1800. The total cost was $232,372.

＊　　＊　　＊

On August 24, 1814, during the War of 1812, British troops invaded Washington and burned the White House in retaliation for an earlier burning of Canadian government buildings in York, Ontario, by the United States forces. The English soldiers reportedly ate a dinner prepared for the President at the White House, and then torched the building, destroying all but the outer walls. At the urging of President Madison, Congress decided to rebuild the public buildings in Washington rather than move the capital to another city. James Hoban returned to reconstruct the President's House as it had been before the fire. The weakened walls were dismantled to the basement level on the east and west sides and on the north except for the central section. Most of the carved ornamentation, bearing the scorch marks of the fire, was reused. President James Monroe moved into a new house in the autumn of 1817.

＊　　＊　　＊

In 1792, James Hoban had proposed a south porch with doors opening to it from the three south parlors. It was never built. In 1817, Benjamin Latrobe drew proposals for north and south porticoes. The south portico was not constructed until 1824 and the north portico not until 1829 and then under the supervision of James Hoban. Both porticoes (the south is really a porch) are made of Seneca sandstone from Maryland. Only after Andrew Jackson's election in 1828 did

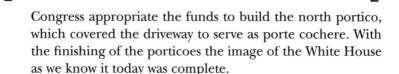

Congress appropriate the funds to build the north portico, which covered the driveway to serve as porte cochere. With the finishing of the porticoes the image of the White House as we know it today was complete.

✤ ✤ ✤

The White House was the largest house in the United States until after the Civil War.

✤ ✤ ✤

The White House is 168 feet long.

✤ ✤ ✤

The White House is 85 feet 6 inches wide without porticoes—152 feet wide with porticoes.

✤ ✤ ✤

The overall height of the White House (to the top of the roof) is 70 feet on the south and 60 feet 4 inches on the north; the facade (grade of lawn to parapet) is 60 feet on the south (lawn at 54 feet above sea level) and 50 feet 4 inches on the north.

✤ ✤ ✤

The White House sits on 18 acres of land.

✤ ✤ ✤

The White House has 132 rooms, including 16 family-guest rooms, 1 main kitchen, 1 diet kitchen, 1 family kitchen, and 31 bathrooms.

✤ ✤ ✤

The White House has (excluding storage rooms): 10 rooms on the Ground Floor, 1 main corridor, 6 restrooms; 8 rooms on the State Floor, 1 main corridor, 1 entrance hall; 16 rooms,

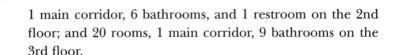

1 main corridor, 6 bathrooms, and 1 restroom on the 2nd floor; and 20 rooms, 1 main corridor, 9 bathrooms on the 3rd floor.

❖ ❖ ❖

The White House tennis court was built in 1902 behind the West Wing, but was moved to the west side of the south lawn in 1909 to make way for the expansion of Executive office space.

❖ ❖ ❖

A heated indoor swimming pool was built in 1933 for Franklin D. Roosevelt's therapy—he suffered from the effects of polio. During President Nixon's first term, this space in the West Wing was converted into the White House pressroom. The Ford administration installed an outdoor pool on the South lawn in 1975.

❖ ❖ ❖

Bowling lanes were first built in 1947 in the basement of the West Wing but were moved to the Old Executive Office Building in 1955. In 1969, President and Mrs. Nixon, both avid bowlers, had a one-lane alley built in an underground workspace area below the driveway.

❖ ❖ ❖

A small movie theater, converted from a long cloakroom, was installed in the East Wing in 1942.

❖ ❖ ❖

A game room with billiard and Ping-Pong tables was constructed in 1970 on the third floor of the White House.

❖ ❖ ❖

During President Clinton's first term, a jogging track was built around the driveway of the south grounds.

❖   ❖   ❖

President Eisenhower had a putting green installed outside the Oval Office with a small sand trap on one side. A new practice green was built on the south grounds in 1996.

❖   ❖   ❖

The first bath tubs in the White House were portable and made of tin. There was no running water and it was brought in with buckets.

❖   ❖   ❖

Running water was piped into the White House in 1833.

❖   ❖   ❖

Gaslighting was installed in the White House in 1848, replacing candles and oil lamps.

❖   ❖   ❖

Central heating was installed in the White House in 1837, at a time when most of the country kept warm with a log or coal fire.

❖   ❖   ❖

Running hot water was first installed into the first family's second floor bathroom in 1853.

❖   ❖   ❖

A cooking stove replaced the kitchen's open-hearth fireplace for preparing meals in 1801.

❖   ❖   ❖

In 1881, a hydraulic elevator was installed the White House; in 1898, its first electric elevator was put in.

✤ ✤ ✤

In 1866, a telegraph office was installed in the White House.

✤ ✤ ✤

The staff of the White House first started using typewriters in 1880.

✤ ✤ ✤

In 1891, electricity was brought into in the White House.

✤ ✤ ✤

In 1925, President Coolidge was the first president to make a radio broadcast from the White House.

✤ ✤ ✤

During the Great Depression, President Franklin Roosevelt broadcast his famous fireside chats from the Diplomatic Reception Room.

✤ ✤ ✤

Electric vacuum cleaners were used for the first time on White House carpets in 1922.

✤ ✤ ✤

The White House acquired its first electric refrigerator in 1926.

✤ ✤ ✤

Air conditioning was first installed in the White House's private quarters in 1933.

✤ ✤ ✤

President Truman often used the White House as a film backdrop for presidential addresses. In 1952, he also hosted a televised tour of the newly renovated White House with news reporter Walter Cronkite.

❧ ❧ ❧

In 1955, President Eisenhower gave the first televised presidential news conference. The first live televised news conference was broadcast during the Kennedy administration.

❧ ❧ ❧

John Tyler was the first president to marry while in office.

❧ ❧ ❧

In 1886, Grover Cleveland became the only president to be married in a White House ceremony. He married Frances Folsom, the twenty-one-year-old daughter of a former law partner.

❧ ❧ ❧

The first president to have an official White House automobile was William Howard Taft.

❧ ❧ ❧

Benjamin Harrison brought the first Christmas tree inside the White House in 1889.

❧ ❧ ❧

The Gilbert Stuart portrait of George Washington, obtained in 1800, is the oldest remaining possession of the White House.

❧ ❧ ❧

During the War of 1812, the Gilbert Stuart portrait of George Washington was saved by Dolley Madison before the British troops burned the White House.

Thomas Jefferson once described the Presidency as "a splendid misery" and Andrew Jackson called it "dignified slavery."

❖   ❖   ❖

The egalitarian minded President Thomas Jefferson disliked ceremony. He replaced the custom of bowing to greet guests at the White House with the more democratic practice of shaking hands.

❖   ❖   ❖

In 1812, Dolley Madison arranged the first wedding to be held at the White House, that of Lucy Payne Washington, her widowed sister, to Thomas Todd, a Supreme Court Justice.

❖   ❖   ❖

In 1881, after President Garfield was shot by an office-seeking fanatic, a metal detecting device invented by Alexander Graham Bell was used to try to locate a bullet. The bed's steel springs were not removed as Bell ordered and the attempt failed to find the bullet and save the president's life.

❖   ❖   ❖

On February 25, 1828, John Adams, the grandson of the second president and son of President John Quincy Adams, married Mary Catherine Hellen in the White House. The event marks the only time that a president's son has been married in the executive mansion.

❖   ❖   ❖

After Andrew Jackson's inaugural address at the Capitol, a crowd of thousands descended on the White House to enjoy the reception for the "People's President." But the crowd turned rowdy and they began to destroy White House china, glassware, and furnishings. To escape the uncontrollable crowd of merrymakers and handshakers, President Jackson was forced to leave through a window.

During the Hayes administration, no alcoholic beverages were served at any function. It was a prohibition that earned the First Lady Lucretia Hayes the nickname of "Lemonade Lucy."

✤   ✤   ✤

Abigail Fillmore, a former schoolteacher, obtained congressional funds in 1850 for the first official library in the Executive Mansion.

✤   ✤   ✤

Eight Chief Executives have died in office: Zachary Taylor, William Henry Harrison, Warren G. Harding, Franklin Delano Roosevelt; and four of them by assassination—Abraham Lincoln, James A. Garfield, William McKinley, and John F. Kennedy.

✤   ✤   ✤

President Abraham Lincoln's autopsy was conducted by two pathologists and seven doctors in the Prince of Wales Room on the second floor of the White House, shortly after he died—the victim of an assassin's bullet—on the morning of April 15, 1865.

✤   ✤   ✤

A clerk-typist, a woman, first appeared on the White House staff payroll in 1889, when Benjamin Harrison came to office.

✤   ✤   ✤

President Warren G. Harding regularly hosted poker parties in the White House during his administration (1921–1923).

✤   ✤   ✤

All of the presidents from Ulysses S. Grant to Chester A. Arthur wore beards. Cleveland broke the custom, although he did wear a mustache.

Because it was a commonly believed at that time that flowers gave off unhealthy vapors and absorbed valuable elements from the air, very few cut flowers were used in the White House during the Polk administration.

❖   ❖   ❖

First Lady Dolley Madison is considered to have introduced social dancing to the White House, most notably the Waltz, which critics at that time called "the hugging process set to music."

❖   ❖   ❖

In 1801, the United States Marine Band played at the first reception at the White House on New Year's Day, and ever since they have performed regularly. From the time of Jefferson, the band has been known as "The President's Own."

❖   ❖   ❖

The first black artist to have performed at the White House was Thomas Green Bethune, nicknamed "Blind Tom." He played the piano for President James Buchanan in 1859. Although mentally retarded, accounts from the period reported that he was a phenomenal prodigy who was said to have played like Mozart, Beethoven or Gottschalk.

❖   ❖   ❖

Ulysses S. Grant once remarked about his musical knowledge: I know only two tunes—one is Yankee Doodle and the other isn't."

❖   ❖   ❖

The first president to occupy the White House was John Adams in 1800, and one of his first additions was a vegetable garden.

❖   ❖   ❖

In 1801, Thomas Jefferson was also active in planning improvements for the White House garden, including a stone wall

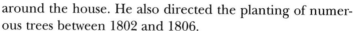

around the house. He also directed the planting of numerous trees between 1802 and 1806.

❖   ❖   ❖

While the White House was being rebuilt after the 1814 fire, James Monroe increased tree plantings on the grounds based on plans by architect Charles Bulfinch.

❖   ❖   ❖

Pennsylvania Avenue did not originally cross in front of the White House. The area was a public ground used for fairs and parades. In 1822 the avenue was cut through the north side of the President's Park and soon thereafter Lafayette Park was established.

❖   ❖   ❖

The federal government used Charles Bulfinch's planting scheme for a thick grove of trees for the square north of the White House and named the park in honor of General Lafayette in 1824–1825.

❖   ❖   ❖

In 1825, John Quincy Adams planted the first flower garden on White House grounds and also put in ornamental trees.

❖   ❖   ❖

Andrew Jackson created the White House orangery—an early type of greenhouse—where tropical fruit trees and flowers were grown. He also added more trees, including the famous Jackson magnolia, to the White House grounds in 1835.

❖   ❖   ❖

President James K. Polk placed a bronze statue of Thomas Jefferson by David d'Engers on the North Lawn in 1848. The

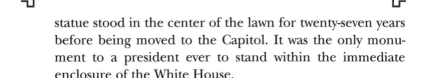

statue stood in the center of the lawn for twenty-seven years before being moved to the Capitol. It was the only monument to a president ever to stand within the immediate enclosure of the White House.

✤   ✤   ✤

Sculptor Clark Mills's famous equestrian statue of Andrew Jackson was unveiled in the center of Lafayette Park in 1853.

✤   ✤   ✤

In 1857, workers demolished the White House orangery to make way for a new wing for the Treasury Department; a replacement greenhouse was constructed on the west side of the White House, adjoining the State Floor.

✤   ✤   ✤

East and West Executive Avenues were built on each side of the White House as public streets in 1866 and 1871.

✤   ✤   ✤

In 1867, the West Wing conservatory was destroyed by fire. Architect Alfred B. Mullet designed and built a more fireproof iron frame and wood sash replacement.

✤   ✤   ✤

In the 1870s, President Grant had a billiard room built between the greenhouse and the mansion.

✤   ✤   ✤

In the 1870s, Ulysses S. Grant directed the expansion of the grounds to the south and built round pools on the North and South lawns.

✤   ✤   ✤

From 1878 to 1880, during the administration of Rutherford B.

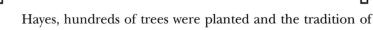

Hayes, hundreds of trees were planted and the tradition of planting commemorative trees was inaugurated.

❖   ❖   ❖

Stables were an important part of early White House life. First located several blocks from the Executive Mansion, they were shifted around until the creation of greenhouses forced their removal in 1869 from the west colonnade to the area southwest of the President's Grounds.

❖   ❖   ❖

Chester A. Arthur, president from 1881 to 1885, did not feel the White House was adequately furnished. He called on Louis C. Tiffany, famous for creating fashionable interiors in New York, to add his touch to the White House. Tiffany worked in the East, Blue, and Red Rooms; the State Dining Room, and the transverse corridor, all on the state floor. By far the greatest cost of Tiffany's redecoration was in artistic painting. Practically every surface was transformed with his decorative patterns. His trademark colored glass and complicated glazing accented the transverse hall and entrance hall by . "Twenty-four wagon loads of old furniture and junk from the White House" were sent to warehouse and sold for $8000 in 1882. But in reality what was sold was priceless.

❖   ❖   ❖

One of Theodore Roosevelt's earliest acts as president was to issue an order establishing the "White House" as the building's official name. Previously, it had been called the "President's House" or the "Executive Mansion." In 1902, Mrs. Roosevelt asked the distinguished architect Charles McKim for his recommendations for a complete renovation of the house which led to major changes in the interior and in the functioning of the building. It doubled the space allocated to the family living quarters, provided a new wing for the president

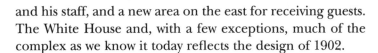
and his staff, and a new area on the east for receiving guests. The White House and, with a few exceptions, much of the complex as we know it today reflects the design of 1902.

❖　　❖　　❖

The Rose Garden, nearly a century old and redesigned several times, reflects the charm and flavor of early American gardens. Ellen Axson Wilson, first wife of Woodrow Wilson (1913–1921) planted the first rose garden in the manner of seventeenth-century Italian gardens. A long, hedge bordered "president's walk" was built to the executive office, along the Jefferson colonnade. The Rose Garden today reflects its redesign in 1961 for President and Mrs. John F. Kennedy. It functions as an outdoor space for gatherings and accommodates several hundred spectators.

❖　　❖　　❖

The White House had always had an attic, but a full third floor was not created until the Coolidge Administration, when problems with the roof structure were discovered. Recommendations were made to replace the old roof and timber structure. In 1927 William Adams Delano of the New York firm of Adams and Delano was called upon for consultation. After studying Hoban's 1793 drawing, he increased the pitch of the roof and lowered the floor to accommodate new guest and service rooms beneath a steel and concrete roof structure. At Mrs. Coolidge's request, a sunroom facing south toward the river, the predecessor of the current solarium was added.

❖　　❖　　❖

The term "West Wing" did not come into common usage until the 1930s. A "temporary office building" had been built in 1902 for the president and his staff, but Theodore Roosevelt continued to use an office in the residence as well. In 1909,

President Taft had the West Wing enlarged and made permanent, adding an oval office. Herbert Hoover remodeled the wing and rebuilt it after a fire in 1929.

❖ ❖ ❖

With the expansion of the staff in the 1930s, Franklin D. Roosevelt requested additional space, and the wing was completely rebuilt under the eye of Eric Gugler. He built a second story, excavated a larger basement for staff and support services, and moved the oval office from the south to its present location in the southeast corner, adjacent to the Rose Garden.

❖ ❖ ❖

At the request of President Franklin D. Roosevelt, Lorenzo Winslow, a government architect assigned to the White House, prepared designs and supervised construction in 1942 of a new east wing. In 1902, McKim constructed a new glass-enclosed wing on its foundations and created an entrance for social functions with a port cochere for guests and carriages. There were no changes to the wing for forty years. The new east wing contained a formal entrance for guests, offices on the first and second floors, and an air raid shelter underground.

❖ ❖ ❖

THE VERMEIL ROOM, is also called the Gold Room. It serves as a display room and as a ladies sitting room for formal occasions. The walls of the paneled room are soft yellow and complements the collection of vermeil, or gilded silver.

❖ ❖ ❖

THE WHITE HOUSE LIBRARY was originally, according to the first official inventory in February 1801, the cluttered Room 17 of the basement filled with "Tubs Buckets and a variety of

Lumber." The room served as a laundry area until Theodore Roosevelt's renovation of the Ground Floor in 1902, when it was renamed the "Gentlemen's Ante-Room." In 1935, it was remodeled as a library, and selected works representative of the full spectrum of American thought and tradition were collected for the use of the President and his staff. The Library is furnished in the style of the late Federal period (1800–1820).

❖   ❖   ❖

THE CHINA ROOM, formerly the "Presidential Collection Room," displays the ever-growing collection of White House china. The room has a red color scheme to match the nearby portrait of Mrs. Calvin Coolidge. Almost every past president is represented in the China Room either by state or family china or glassware. The collection is arranged chronologically.

❖   ❖   ❖

THE DIPLOMATIC RECEPTION ROOM serves as the entrance to the White House from South Grounds for the family and for ambassadors arriving to present their credentials to the president. The area in the past has had less glamorous uses: as a boiler and furnace room. It was also the site of President Franklin D. Roosevelt's fireside chats. Since 1960, the room has been furnished as a drawing room of the Federal Period (1790–1820).

❖   ❖   ❖

THE MAP ROOM was used by President Franklin D. Roosevelt as a situation room to follow the course of World War II. It is now a private meeting room for the president or the first lady. It is decorated as a sitting room in the Chippendale style, which flourished in America during the last half of the eighteenth century.

THE EAST ROOM has been the scene of many historic White House events, and was originally designated as the "Public Audience Room." It contains little furniture and is used for large gatherings, such as after-dinner entertainments, concerts, funerals, press conferences, and bill-signing ceremonies. The room is decorated in the late eighteenth-century classical style. The full-length portrait of George Washington that hangs here is one of several copies made by Gilbert Stuart of his "Landsdowne" portrait. It is the only object known to have remained in the White House since 1800. In April of 1865 the East Room was filled with mourners surrounding the body of President Lincoln after he had been assassinated by John Wilkes Booth. Seven presidents have lain in state in the East Room, including John F. Kennedy in November 1963.

❖   ❖   ❖

THE GREEN ROOM was intended to be the "Common Dining Room," but has served various purposes. It was first used as a "Lodging Room." Thomas Jefferson used it as a dining room with a "canvas floor cloth, painted green." James Madison made it a sitting room since his Cabinet met in the East Room next door, and the Monroes used it as the "Card Room" with two tables.

❖   ❖   ❖

THE BLUE ROOM has always been used as a reception room except for a brief period during the administration of John Adams when it served as the south entrance hall. When President Monroe redecorated the "large oval room," he used the French Empire style, which is the present decor. The color blue was first acquired during the administration of Martin Van Buren in 1837.

❖   ❖   ❖

The Red Room is one of four state reception rooms in the White House. The room once served as "the President's Antichamber" for the Cabinet Room or President's Library next door. During the Madison Administration, it became the scene of Dolley Madison's fashionable Wednesday night receptions as the "Yellow Drawing Room." It is furnished in the Empire style of 1810–1830.

❖   ❖   ❖

The State Dining Room can seat as many as 140 guests. It was originally much smaller and served at various times as a drawing room, office, and Cabinet Room. It was not until the administration of Andrew Jackson that it was called the "State Dining Room."

❖   ❖   ❖

The Oval Office is the heart of the West Wing, a room that has become synonymous with the presidency itself. It was not part of the original plan of the 1902 West Wing, but was part of the 1909 expansion of the West Wing. Rumors circulated that the office was oval because Taft, the president in office, had a rather rotund figure.

❖   ❖   ❖

The Lincoln Bedroom is part of a suite of rooms on the second floor of the White House, and serves as a memorial to the martyred president. The most famous piece of furniture in the room is the dark rosewood bed with a high, ornate headboard. A desk he also used is here, which displays Abraham Lincoln's famous Gettysburg Address, signed and dated in his own hand.

❖   ❖   ❖

The Presidents

GEORGE WASHINGTON (1789–1797)

- George Washington had to borrow money to go to his own inauguration.

- Washington was the first president to appear on a postage stamp.

- Washington was one of two presidents that signed the U.S. Constitution.

- Washington was the only president elected unanimously, receiving all 69 of the electoral votes cast.

- At his inauguration, Washington had only one tooth. He wore dentures made of human or animal teeth, ivory or lead, but not wood as legend has it.

- Washington refused to wear a powdered wig, which was high fashion in the late 1700s. Instead, he powdered his red-brown hair and tied it in a short braid down his back.

- Washington carried a portable sundial.

- Washington's inauguration speech was 183 words long and took 90 seconds to read. This was because of his false teeth.

- The six white horses in Washington's stables had their teeth brushed every morning on Washington's orders.

- The nation's capital was located in Philadelphia during Washington's administration, making him the only president

who didn't live in Washington, D.C. during his presidency.

- Washington's face was scarred from smallpox.
- Washington was the only president to die in the eighteenth century.
- George Washington had two ice cream freezers installed at his home in Mount Vernon.
- George Washington left no direct descendant. Though his wife Martha had four children by a previous marriage, Washington never had biological offspring to continue his line.
- Washington's shoe size was thirteen.
- Washington's IQ was estimated to be about 125.
- He was a very loud snorer.
- His last words (to his aide, Tobias Lear): "I am just going. Have me decently buried and do not let my body be put into a vault in less than two days after I am dead. Do you understand me? . . . 'Tis well."

JOHN ADAMS (1797–1801)

- Adams was the first president to live in the White House. He and his family moved in in November 1800 while the paint was still wet.
- Adams was one of two presidents to sign the Declaration of Independence.
- John Adams was a second cousin to Samuel Adams, and a third cousin to his own wife, Abigail Smith Adams.
- Adams was one of three presidents not to attend the inauguration of his successor. Not only was Adams disappointed in losing to Jefferson, he was also grieving the death of his son Charles.
- Adams was the great-great-grandson of John and Priscilla

Alden, Pilgrims who landed at Plymouth Rock in 1620.

- Adams lived longer than any other president at his death. When he died he was 90 years, 247 days old.

- The only presidents to sign the Declaration of Independence, Adams and Jefferson both died on its fiftieth anniversary, July 4, 1826. Adams' dying words were "Thomas Jefferson still . . . . survives." Jefferson, however, had passed on a few hours earlier.

THOMAS JEFFERSON (1801–1809)

- Jefferson was the first president to shake hands instead of bow to people.

- Thomas Jefferson was the first president to have a grandchild born in the White House.

- Jefferson was one of two presidents who signed the Declaration of Independence.

- Jefferson's library of approximately 6,000 books became the basis of the Library of Congress. His books were purchased from him for $23,950.

- Jefferson kept a mockingbird named Dick in the White House study, and let the bird ride on his shoulder whenever possible. President Jefferson even trained Dick to take bits of food that he held between his lips at meals. When Jefferson went upstairs, his faithful companion would hop up after him, step after step, never far from his side.

- Jefferson was the first president to be inaugurated in Washington, D.C.

- Bears brought back from Lewis and Clark's famous expedition were displayed in cages on the White House lawn. For years the White House was sometimes referred to as the "president's bear garden."

- Jefferson played the violin.

- He suggested the decimal system of money we use.
- He wrote over 20,000 letters in his lifetime.
- Jefferson founded, designed and built the University of Virginia.
- Jefferson owned 200 slaves.
- Jefferson is credited with several inventions, including the swivel chair, a pedometer, a machine to make fiber from hemp, a letter-copying machine, and the lazy susan.
- His last words: "Is it the Fourth? I resign my spirit to God, my daughter to my country."

JAMES MADISON (1809–1817)

- Madison was our smallest president, weighing 100 pounds, and standing 5 feet and 4 inches tall.
- James Madison was one of two presidents to sign the U.S. Constitution.
- Madison was a half first cousin twice removed of George Washington and a second cousin of Zachary Taylor.
- During the War of 1812 Madison was under enemy fire. He was the first president to be in that situation. Madison was younger than both of his vice presidents, and both of his vice presidents died while they were in office.
- Madison was diagnosed as epileptic.
- Madison was the first U.S. congressman to become president.
- His last words: "I always talk better lying down."

JAMES MONROE (1817–1825)

- The capital of Liberia is Monrovia, named after James Monroe.
- Monroe's daughter, Maria Monroe, was the first daughter of

a president ever to be married in the White House.

- In the election of 1820, Monroe received every electoral vote except one. A New Hampshire delegate wanted Washington to be the only president elected unanimously.

- Monroe's inauguration in 1817 was the first to be held outdoors.

- Monroe was the first president to ride on a steamboat.

- Monroe was the only president to serve in two different cabinet posts. He was secretary of state and war.

- James Monroe was the first president to tour the country.

- Monroe was the first U.S. senator to be elected president.

- Monroe was wounded during the Revolutionary War.

- Monroe's favorite foods were chicken, breads, and biscuits.

John Quincy Adams (1825–1829)

- John Quincy Adams along with George W. Bush are the only sons of a former presidents to also become president.

- His wife, Louisa Catherine Johnson, was the only foreign first lady.

- John Quincy Adams was a second cousin once removed of Samuel Adams and a third cousin once removed to his own mother, Abigail Smith Adams.

- Adams liked to take nude dips in the Potomac River almost every day.

- John Quincy Adams was the only president to be elected to the House of Representatives after serving as president.

- Adams argued before the Supreme Court on behalf of slaves from the ship Amistad who mutinied during their journey from Africa.

- John Quincy Adams owned a pet alligator which he kept in the East Room of the White House.

- Adams was the first president to be photographed.
- One of his sons, George Washington Adams, died at the age of 28, an apparent suicide.
- John Quincy Adams's last words: "This is the end of earth, but I am composed."

Andrew Jackson (1829–1837)

- Jackson was the only president to pay off the national debt.
- Jackson was the first president to ride in a train.
- On January 30, 1835, a mentally disturbed man named Richard Lawrence fired two different guns at Jackson from point-blank range. Both weapons failed to fire. Jackson then chased after Lawrence and beat him with his cane.
- At his funeral in 1845, his pet parrot had to be removed because it was swearing.
- Jackson was the only president to have been held as a prisoner of war. This was during the Revolutionary War. Jackson was only 13 years old at the time.
- He was the only president to serve in both the Revolutionary War and the War of 1812.
- During his lifetime, Jackson was involved in many duels. His most vicious and bloody was on May 30, 1806. Jackson fought with Charles Dickinson over some things that he said about Jackson's wife. Dickinson shot Jackson directly in the chest, about two inches from his heart. But Jackson didn't fall down, but he raised his gun and killed Dickinson. He then walked away, but the bullet lodged too close to his heart to be removed and he carried it for the rest of his life.
- Andrew Jackson was orphaned at the age of fourteen.
- Jackson was the first president born in a log cabin.

- His last words: "Both white and black . . . Oh, do not cry. Be good children, and we shall all meet in heaven."

MARTIN VAN BUREN (1837–1841)

- Van Buren was the first president born after the Declaration of Independence was signed. He was the first president born as a United States citizen.

- The term "It's O.K." came from Van Buren, who grew up in Kinderhook, New York. After he went into politics, he became known by the nickname "Old Kinderhook." Soon people were saying "Is it OK?" referring to Van Buren, and the word "okay" was derived.

- His autobiography does not mention his wife once.

- The only president of Dutch ancestry, Van Buren and his wife spoke Dutch at home.

- Van Buren owned two tiger cubs as pets.

- Van Buren's favorite sport was riding horses.

- When he was vice president, he presided over the Senate with loaded pistols.

- His last words: "There is but one reliance."

WILLIAM HENRY HARRISON (1841)

- William Henry Harrison was the first president to die in office, about thirty-two days after he was elected.

- When Harrison was elected president in 1840, the Indian leader Tecumseh placed a curse on him. He said every president elected in a year that ends with a "0" will die while in office. Harrison died while in office, as did Lincoln, elected in 1860, Garfield, elected in 1880, McKinley, elected in 1900, Harding, elected in 1920, Roosevelt, elected in 1940,

and Kennedy, elected in 1960. Reagan, elected in 1980, broke the curse, but was almost assassinated while in office.

- His last words: "I wish you to understand the true principles of the government. I wish them carried out. I ask nothing more."

John Tyler (1841–1845)

- John Tyler was the president to have the most children. He had fifteen.
- John Tyler joined the Confederacy twenty years after he was in office and became the only president named a sworn enemy of the United States. Tyler was the only president to hold office in the Confederacy.
- Tyler's second wife, Julia, initiated the practice of playing "Hail to the Chief" whenever a president appears in public.
- Tyler was the first president whose wife died while he was in office.
- His last words: "Doctor, I am going. . . . Perhaps, it is best."

James Knox Polk (1845–1849)

- Polk was the only president who was also the Speaker of the House of Representatives.
- Polk was the first president to voluntarily retire after one term.
- Polk survived a gallstone operation at age 17 without anesthesia or antiseptics.
- During his term, gaslights were first installed in the White House.

ZACHARY TAYLOR (1849–1850)

- When Taylor was inaugurated in March 1849, he would not take the Oath of Office on a Sunday. The offices of president and vice president were vacant at the time, so someone had to be the president, but who? David Rice Atchison, the President Pro Tempore of the Senate, was sworn in as president. He did not get to do much, when asked, he said, "I went to bed. There had been two or three busy nights finishing up the work of the Senate, and I slept most of that Sunday."

- Taylor spent July 4, 1850, eating cherries and milk at a ceremony at the Washington Monument. He got sick from the heat and died five days later, the second president to die in office.

- Taylor's body was recently exhumed because some thought that his death was caused by murder rather than natural causes.

- Taylor, the twelfth president of the United States, didn't vote until he was sixty-two years old and didn't even vote in his own election because he was a soldier and moved too often to establish legal residency until he retired.

- Taylor kept his old war-horse named Whitney on the White House lawn. People would pluck hairs from it for souvenirs.

- Taylor chewed tobacco and was famous for never missing a spittoon when he spat.

- Taylor rode his horse sidesaddle whenever he went into battle.

- Abraham Lincoln gave the eulogy at his funeral.

- His last words: "I am about to die. I expect the summons very soon. I have tried to discharge my duties faithfully. I regret nothing, but I am sorry that I am about to leave my friends."

MILLARD FILLMORE (1850–1853)

- Fillmore established the first permanent library in the White House.

- Fillmore refused an honorary degree of Doctor of Civil Law from Oxford. He said, "No man should accept a degree that he cannot read."

- Fillmore's wife had the first "running-water bathtub" installed in the White House.

- Fillmore was the last president born in the eighteenth century.

- His last words: "The nourishment is palatable."

FRANKLIN PIERCE (1853–1857)

- Franklin Pierce was the first president to have a Christmas tree in the White House.

- Because of religious considerations, Franklin Pierce is the only president to have said "I promise" instead of "I swear" at his Inauguration.

- Pierce died of cirrhosis of the liver as a result of years of heavy drinking.

- Pierce was arrested while in office for running over an old woman with his horse, but his case was dropped due to insufficient evidence in 1853.

- One of the Democratic party's slogans during Pierce's campaign for president was: "We Polked you in 1844; we shall Pierce you in 1852."

- Pierce installed the first central-heating system in the White House.

- Pierce always insisted that grace be said before a meal.

- During his second year at Bowdoin College in Maine, Pierce had the lowest grades out of anyone in his class. He changed his study habits, and graduated third in his class. Among his

class mates were Nathaniel Hawthorne and Henry Wadsworth Longfellow.

JAMES BUCHANAN (1857–1861)

- Buchanan had the opportunity to buy Cuba for only $90,000,000, but Congress wouldn't let him because they thought he would steal the money and run away.

- Buchanan was the only president to never be married.

- He is said to have the neatest handwriting of all the presidents.

- When England's Prince of Wales came to visit the White House in 1860, so many guests came with him that Buchanan had to sleep in the hallway.

- Buchanan was farsighted in one eye and nearsighted in the other. His left eye also sat higher in its socket than his right. He tipped his head to the left and closed one eye when talking to people.

- He sent a note to newly elected Abe Lincoln saying, "My dear sir, if you are as happy on entering the White House as I on leaving, you are a happy man indeed."

- His last words: "O Lord, God Almighty, as Thou wilt."

ABRAHAM LINCOLN (1861–1865)

- Lincoln was the first president to have a beard while in office. He grew it at the suggestion of an eleven-year-old girl.

- Abe Lincoln's mother, Nancy Hanks Lincoln, died when the family dairy cow ate poisonous mushrooms and she drank the milk.

- A plot was developed to steal Lincoln's body after his assassination, so a secret society to guard his tomb was formed.

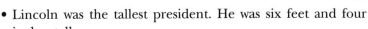

- Lincoln was the tallest president. He was six feet and four inches tall.

- Lincoln once had a dream right before the fall of Richmond that he would die. He dreamed that he was in the White House, he heard crying and when he found the room it was coming from he asked who had died. The man said the president. He looked in the coffin and saw his own face. A week later Lincoln died.

- Lincoln was shot on Good Friday.

- Lincoln had a cat named "Bob," a turkey named "Jack," and a dog named "Jib."

- He was the first president to be photographed at his inauguration. John Wilkes Booth, his assassin, can be seen standing close to Lincoln in the picture.

- Abraham Lincoln was shot while watching a performance of *Our American Cousin* at Ford's Theatre in Washington, D.C. The same play was also running at the McVerick Theatre in Chicago on May 18, 1860, the day Lincoln was nominated for president in that city.

- The contents of his pockets on the night of his assassination were not revealed until February 12, 1976. They contained two pairs of spectacles; a chamois lens cleaner; an ivory and silver pocketknife; a large white Irish linen handkerchief with "A. Lincoln" embroidered in red; a gold quartz watch fob without a watch; a new silk-lined, leather wallet containing a pencil, a Confederate five-dollar bill, and news clippings of unrest in the Confederate army, emancipation in Missouri, the Union party platform of 1864, and an article on the presidency by John Bright.

- Lincoln and his wife held seances in the White House. They had great interest in psychic phenomena.

- Lincoln was the first president to die by assassination.

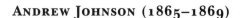

ANDREW JOHNSON (1865–1869)

- Johnson was drunk at his inauguration for vice president.(His doctor had prescribed him some alcoholic medicine.)

- He was the only president elected to U.S. Senate after his presidential term.

- Andrew Johnson was a self-educated tailor. He is the only president who made his own clothes as well as his cabinet's.

- He was the first president to be impeached.

ULYSSES SIMPSON GRANT (1869–1877)

- Grant was one of three presidents to graduate from a military academy, he went to West Point.

- He finished his autobiography only a few weeks before his death from cancer. The book provided an income of $500,000 for his family after his death.

- While president, Ulysses S. Grant was arrested for driving his horse too fast. He was fined $20.

- His real name was Hiram Ulysses Grant. He changed it because he didn't want to enter West Point with initials like H.U.G.

- Grant ate a cucumber soaked in vinegar for breakfast each day.

- Grant was the first president to have both parents alive when he took office.

- Grant smoked ten to twenty cigars a day. A reporter reported that Grant liked cigars, and people started to send him cigars. He received over 20,000 of them.

- Ten years after he was president, Grant was stricken with throat cancer, and he regularly swabbed his throat with cocaine, becoming addicted to it.

- Grant was the second man in American history to be a Lieutenant General.

- Ulysses S. Grant had the boyhood nickname "Useless."

- Upon graduation, Grant had no intention of keeping the military as his career and planned instead on being a professor of mathematics.

- On August 28, 1848, Grant married Julia Dent from St. Louis, whose family held slaves. Grant himself owned a slave named William Jones, acquired from his father-in-law. At a time when he could have desperately used the money from the sale of Jones, Grant signed a document that gave him his freedom.

- On the day Lincoln was assassinated, Grant's wife Julia was stalked by John Wilkes Booth. If the general had accepted the invitation to go to Ford's Theater with the presidential party, there may have been a double tragedy. They went instead to Burlington, New Jersey, to see their children.

- His last words: "Water."

RUTHERFORD BIRCHARD HAYES (1877–1881)

- Hayes was the first president to use a telephone while in office. The first telephone was installed in the White House in 1879.

- Of the five presidents who served in the Civil War, Hayes was the only one to be wounded.

- He won the presidency by only one electoral vote.

- His wife, Lucy Hayes, was known as "Lemonade Lucy" because she banned alcohol, smoking, dancing, and card playing from the White House.

- Hayes and his wife conducted the first Easter egg roll on the White House lawn.

- He was named after his father, Rutherford Hayes, and his

mother, Sophia Birchard.

- Hayes was the first president to graduate from law school.

- His last words: "I know that I am going where Lucy (his wife) is."

JAMES ABRAM GARFIELD (1881)

- James Garfield could write Latin with one hand and Greek with the other.

- A book published in 1940 contained 370 proofs of the Pythagorean Theorem, including one by Garfield.

- Garfield was the second president shot in office. Doctors tried to find the bullet with a metal detector invented by Alexander Graham Bell. But the device failed because Garfield was placed on a bed with metal springs, and no one thought to move him. He died on September 19, 1881.

- Garfield was our first left-handed president.

- On election day, November 2, 1880, he was at the same time a member of the House, senator-elect and president-elect.

- His last words: "Swaim (his chief of staff David G. Swaim), can't you stop this? Oh, Swaim!"

CHESTER ALAN ARTHUR (1881–1885)

- Arthur sold twenty-six wagons full of White House furniture for about eight thousand dollars. What he did not know was that the furniture was priceless.

- His favorite food was mutton chops.

- Arthur was the first president to take the Oath of Office in his own home.

- Arthur's citizenship was questioned when political opponents alleged that he was born across the Vermont border in Canada. Arthur denied this and continued on with his term.

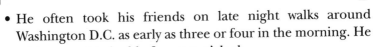

- He often took his friends on late night walks around Washington D.C. as early as three or four in the morning. He seldom went to bed before two o'clock.

Grover Cleveland (1885–1889, 1893–1897)

- He was the only president to be elected to two nonconsecutive terms.
- Cleveland was the first president to be filmed. In 1895, Alexander Black came to Washington and asked Cleveland to appear in "A Capital Courtship", his photoplay. He agreed to be filmed while signing a bill into law. "A Captial Courtship" was a big hit on the Lyceum Circuit.
- Cleveland was the only president to be married in the White House and was the first to have a child born there.
- The Baby Ruth candy bar was named after Cleveland's baby daughter, Ruth.
- Cleveland used his veto powers five hundred and eighty-four times during his two terms. This is the highest total of any president except Franklin Roosevelt, who served three terms.
- Grover Cleveland went sailing during July 1893 for what people thought was a fishing trip, but he was really having surgery for a cancerous growth in his mouth. The operation was kept so secret that nobody found out about it until 1917.
- Cleveland answered the White House phone, personally.
- His last words: "I have tried so hard to do right."

Benjamin Harrison (1889–1893)

- Harrison was the grandson of William Henry Harrison.
- He was the first president to use electricity in the White

House. After he got an electrical shock, his family often refused to touch the light switches. Sometimes they would go to bed leaving all the White House lights on.

- He was known as the "Human Iceberg" because he was stiff and formal when dealing with people.

- The wearing of kid gloves to protect his hands from skin infection earned him the nickname of "Kid Gloves" Harrison.

- His last words: "Are the doctors here? Doctor . . . my lungs."

WILLIAM MCKINLEY (1897–1901)

- McKinley was the first president to ride in an automobile. He rode in an electric ambulance to the hospital after he was shot.

- After being shot, he saw the shooter being beaten to the ground, he then cried, "Don't let them hurt him!"

- McKinley was the first president to campaign by telephone.

- McKinley always wore a red carnation in his lapel for good luck.

- McKinley's commanding officer in the Civil War was Rutherford B. Hayes.

- McKinley kept a parrot in the White House that could whistle "Yankee Doodle." McKinley would whistle the first part, and the bird would finish it.

- His last words: "It is God's way. His will, not ours, be done."

THEODORE ROOSEVELT (1901–1909)

- Roosevelt wanted the motto "In God We Trust" removed from the new $20 gold coin designed in 1907. Roosevelt

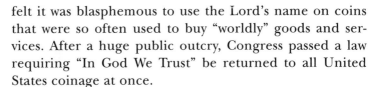

felt it was blasphemous to use the Lord's name on coins that were so often used to buy "worldly" goods and services. After a huge public outcry, Congress passed a law requiring "In God We Trust" be returned to all United States coinage at once.

- He was the first president to ride in an airplane. He flew for four minutes in a plane built by the Wright Brothers on October 11, 1910.

- Theodore Roosevelt was our youngest president—he was younger than Kennedy at the time that McKinley was assassinated and he was inaugurated.

- In 1912, Roosevelt took a drink of coffee and exclaimed, "That coffee tastes good, even to the last drop!" Maxwell House got their motto from this.

- He won the Nobel Peace Prize in 1906 for his role of peacemaker in the Russo-Japanese War. He was the first American to ever win the award.

- Theodore Roosevelt was shot on October 14, 1912 just before giving a speech during his run as "Bull Moose" candidate. Even though the bullet entered his lung, he still gave the speech!

- The teddy bear is named after Theodore Roosevelt.

- Roosevelt was blind in his left eye. He lost his eyesight when he was boxing.

- His favorite word was "bully" meaning great.

- Roosevelt had a photographic memory. He could read a page in the time it took anyone else to read a sentence.

- He was the first president to be popularly referred to by his initials, TR.

- His last words: "Please put out the light."

WILLIAM HOWARD TAFT (1909–1913)

- Taft is the only president to also serve as Chief Justice in the Supreme Court.

- Taft was the first president to throw the first baseball of a season.

- He was the first president to own a car. He had the stables converted into a four-car garage.

- William H. Taft is one of two presidents who is buried in the Arlington National Cemetery.

- He called the White House "the loneliest place in the world."

- His funeral was the first to be broadcast on the radio.

- Taft was our heaviest president, weighing 332 pounds. He once got stuck in the White House bath tub, so a new one was installed, big enough to hold four grown men.

WOODROW WILSON (1913–1921)

- Wilson was the first president to hold a press conference.

- He won the Nobel Peace Prize in 1920 for his efforts in seeking peace after World War I and supporting the League of Nations.

- Wilson detonated the final explosives to clear the Panama Canal. He sent the signal all the way from New York.

- Wilson was the first president to have earned a Ph.D.

- Wilson couldn't read until he was 9 years old.

- After he suffered a stroke which paralyzed his left side, Edith Wilson, his wife, was his connection with the outside world. She is considered the most powerful first lady there ever was.

- His last words: "I am a broken piece of machinery. When the machinery is broken . . . I am ready."

Warren Gamaliel Harding (1921–1923)

- Harding was the first president to speak over the radio.

- He suffered nervous breakdowns at the age of 24 and had to spend some time in a sanitarium.

- Harding played poker at least twice a week. He once gambled away an entire set of White House china, dating back to Benjamin Harrison's time. His advisors were given the nickname of the "Poker Cabinet" because they all played poker together.

- Out of all the presidents, Harding had the biggest feet. He wore size fourteen shoes.

- He was the first newspaper publisher to be elected president.

- Harding reportedly had been having secret affairs with two women, one of them the young mother of his seven-month-old illegitimate daughter, when he was picked as Republican nominee.

- President Harding died three years into his term, just as news of kickbacks and favoritism involving members of his administration—including the campaign manager he had appointed attorney general—were beginning to become public. Several of his closest advisers had already quit, and two committed suicide, under the weight of a variety of corruption charges. The primary disgrace involved the transferral of naval oil reserves in Teapot Dome, Wyoming, into private hands by the Secretary of the Interior in exchange for $400,000 in bribes.

- News of the Teapot Dome scandal began to break as Harding and his wife were returning from a vacation in Alaska. Harding began to show signs of food poisoning and fatigue, developed pneumonia, and died suddenly. His wife, who some speculated had poisoned him, refused to permit an autopsy. The official cause of death was purported to have been a stroke or heart attack.

- His last words: "That's good. Go on; read some more." (His wife was reading to him from the *Saturday Evening Post*.)

CALVIN COOLIDGE (1923–1929)

- Coolidge's family spoke in sign language when they did not wish to be overheard.

- Calvin Coolidge, a man of few words, was so famous for saying so little that a White House dinner guest made a bet that she could get the president to say more than two words. She told the president of her wager. His reply: "You lose."

- Coolidge had an electronic horse installed in the White House which he rode almost every day.

- Calvin Coolidge was sworn into office by his own father, who was a justice of the peace, at 2:47 in the morning. Coolidge then went back to sleep.

HERBERT CLARK HOOVER (1929–1933)

- Hoover was the first president to have an asteroid named for him.

- The Hoovers spoke in Chinese when they didn't want anyone to overhear what they were talking about.

- Herbert Hoover was one of two presidents to live to be over ninety years old.

- Hoover worked in Australia at the turn of the twentieth century as a mining engineer.

- Hoover was the first president born west of the Mississippi River.

- Hoover approved "The Star-Spangled Banner" as the national anthem.

- He was the youngest member of Stanford University's first graduating class.

- During Prohibition Hoover would visit the Belgian Embassy in Washington D.C. for drinks. It was considered foreign soil, so drinking was legal there.

FRANKLIN DELANO ROOSEVELT (1933–1945)

- Roosevelt was the first president to appear on television.
- There was an assassination attempt on Roosevelt in February 1933. Roosevelt was unharmed, but Anton Cermak, mayor of Chicago, was killed.
- Franklin D. Roosevelt was in office longer than any other president. He served three consecutive terms and died during his fourth.
- Roosevelt's favorite food was fried cornmeal mush.
- He was the first president whose mother was eligible to vote for him.
- Roosevelt had a dog named "Fala" who was with him all the time. He also had a German shepherd named "Major" that was famous for biting several politicians.
- Franklin D. Roosevelt's favorite sport was swimming.
- His last words: "I have a terrific headache."

HARRY S. TRUMAN (1945–1953)

- Harry S Truman was playing poker when he learned he was to be president.
- He was the first president to travel underwater in a modern submarine.
- His middle name is "S." He said, "I was supposed to be named Harrison Shippe Truman, taking the middle name from my paternal grandfather. Others in my family wanted my middle name to be Solomon, taken from my maternal grandfather. But apparently no agreement could be reached

and my name was recorded and stands simply as Harry S Truman."

- He was the first president to give a speech on television.
- Truman was left handed, but his parents made him write with his right hand.
- Truman popularized the saying, "If you can't stand the heat, stay out of the kitchen."
- Harry S Truman was the first president to take office during wartime.

DWIGHT DAVID EISENHOWER (1953–1961)

- He switched his first and middle names around to avoid confusion between he and his father.
- Eisenhower was one of three presidents to graduate from a military academy. He went to West Point where he graduated sixty-fifth in a class of one-hundred and sixty-five.
- He had a putting green installed on the White House lawn.
- Eisenhower was the first president of all fifty states.
- He was the first president to appear on color television.
- Eisenhower was superstitious. He carried three coins with him for good luck: a silver dollar, a five-guinea gold piece, and a French franc.
- He was also a wonderful cook who specialized in barbecued steaks.
- Eisenhower was the first president licensed to pilot a plane.
- He was the only president to serve in both World Wars.
- He was responsible for putting "under God" into the Pledge of Allegiance.
- His last words: "I've always loved my wife. I've always loved my children. I've always loved my grandchildren. And I have always loved my country."

JOHN FITZGERALD KENNEDY (1961–1963)

- Kennedy was the first president to hold a press conference on television.

- He was the first president to also be a Boy Scout.

- Kennedy was the first Roman Catholic president.

- He was the youngest man elected president, but not our youngest president, Teddy Roosevelt was younger at the time of his inauguration.

- John F. Kennedy is one of two presidents that is buried in Arlington National Cemetery.

- One of his favorite poems was "I Have a Rendezvous With Death" by Alan Seeger.

- Kennedy was the first president born in the twentieth century.

- He won a Pulitzer Prize for his book "Profiles in Courage."

- Kennedy was the only president to appoint a brother to a cabinet post.

- Kennedy commissioned Pierre Salinger to buy and stockpile 1,500 Havana cigars on the eve of signing the Cuban trade embargo.

- His right leg was 3/4 of an inch longer than his left, so he wore corrective shoes to make up for it.

- Kennedy was the first president who had served in the U.S. Navy.

- Kennedy was called Jack by his friends.

LYNDON BAINES JOHNSON (1963–1969)

- Johnson was the only president to take the Oath of Office on an airplane from a woman.

- Once when approached by a reporter who asked him a ques-

tion he didn't like, he replied, "Why do you come and ask me, the leader of the Western world, a chicken-shit question like that?"

- Johnson loved the soda Fresca so much that he had a fountain installed in the Oval Office that would dispense the soda at the push of a button.

- He liked to take visitors on 90 mph rides around his Texas ranch in his Lincoln Continental.

- He rejected his official portrait painting, saying it was "the ugliest thing I ever saw."

RICHARD MILHOUS NIXON (1969–1974)

- Nixon was the first to address the Russian people on Soviet television.

- He had the White House swimming pool filled in to give the press more room to stand when covering White House events.

- Nixon suffered from motion sickness and hay fever.

- Nixon's favorite sport was football. Before Super Bowl VI, Nixon called Miami Dolphins coach, Don Shula, to recommend a play. The play never worked.

- He was our only president to resign from office. His letter of resignation was as follows: "Dear Mr. Secretary: I hearby resign the office of the President of the United States. Sincerely, Richard M. Nixon."

GERALD RUDOLPH FORD (1974–1977)

- Ford was born Leslie Lynch King. He was renamed after his adoptive father, Gerald Rudolph Ford Sr.

- Except in formal signature, he signs his name Jerry Ford.

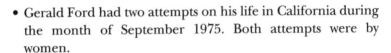

- Gerald Ford had two attempts on his life in California during the month of September 1975. Both attempts were by women.

- Ford was once a male model.

- He became vice president and president without being elected to either office. He became vice president when Spiro T. Agnew, Nixon's elected vice president, resigned. Then Ford became president when Nixon resigned.

- Ford had another swimming pool dug after he became president because Richard Nixon had had the previous one filled in.

- Ford was on the University of Michigan football team from 1931 to 1934. He was offered tryouts by both the Green Bay Packers and the Chicago Bears.

- He is right-handed, but he writes with his left hand.

- When Ford proposed to his wife, he was wearing one brown and one black shoe

- Ford was the first president to have been an Eagle Scout.

- Ford's daughter Susan held her senior prom at the White House.

- Ford was the head boxing coach and assistant football coach at Yale University.

- Ford was one of the members of the Warren Commission appointed to study the assassination of President John F. Kennedy.

- Ford was the first president to pardon a former president.

JAMES EARL CARTER JR. (1977–1981)

- Carter was the first president to be born in a hospital.

- Carter was one of three presidents to attend a military academy. He went to Annapolis, the U.S. Naval Academy.

- Carter studied nuclear physics at Annapolis.

- Carter was the first president sworn in using his nickname, Jimmy.

- Carter only has one testicle.

RONALD WILSON REAGAN (1981–1989)

- Reagan was the oldest president in history. He was 77 when he left office.

- Reagan was the first president who had been divorced.

- He was the only president to be wounded and survive an assassination attempt. Shortly after being shot, Reagan jokingly said, "I forgot to duck."

- Ronald Reagan married his first wife, Jane Wyman, at Forest Lawn Cemetery in Glendale, California.

- Ronald Reagan and his second wife Nancy Davis appeared opposite each other in the movie "Hellcats of the Navy."

- When Ronald Reagan was president and he got his first hearing aid, the sale of hearing aids went up in the United States by 40 percent.

- Sales of jelly beans skyrocketed when Reagan told reporters that he liked them.

GEORGE HERBERT WALKER BUSH (1989–1993)

- Bush played first base for the Yale baseball team.

- When he received his commission in 1943, he became, at nineteen, the youngest pilot then in the Navy, flying fifty-eight combat missions during World War II.

WILLIAM JEFFERSON CLINTON (1993–2001)

- Clinton was the first president to be sued for sexual misconduct and forced to give a deposition while in office.

- Bill Clinton was the first president to have been a Rhodes Scholar.

- Bill Clinton is the only president ever to be elected twice without ever receiving 50 percent of the popular vote. He had 43 percent in 1992 and 49 percent in 1996.

- Bill Clinton is the first left-handed American president to serve two terms.

- He was born William Jefferson Blythe, 4th, after his biological father who was killed a few months before he was born in a car accident. Blythe wasn't hurt badly in the crash, but was knocked unconscious and landed in a deep puddle of water face down, and drowned. Clinton legally changed his last name to that of his stepfather when he was 16.

George W. Bush (2001–   )

- George W. Bush is the second son of a president to be elected to the same office.

- Bush's early life was rather wayward. He was a drinker and seemed more interested in having a good time, rather than pursuing a political career. But around the age of forty, he quit drinking and became more religious, joining the Methodist Church of his wife Laura.

- Bush is the only president to have owned a baseball team. He was a managing partner of the Texas Rangers.

Other Branches of Government

On March 4, 1825, **JOHN QUINCY ADAMS** was inaugurated as president in the Old House Chamber. Later as a member of the House of Representatives, he died in the same room on February 23, 1848.

❖　　　❖　　　❖

THE U.S. CAPITOL BUILDING was the centerpiece of L'Enfant's Plan for Washington. The site L'Enfant chose for the building as atop Jenkins Hill from which radiated broad avenues named for the original states. In 1793, William Thornton, a physician and amateur architect, won the competition to design the building, whose several stages would not be fully completed for decades. George Washington laid the cornerstone of the "Congress House" on September 18, 1793, even though to this day all attempts to find the cornerstone have failed. The Capitol, in its first phase, was an unremarkable building topped with a low dome. Only after the British burned the incomplete building and most of the volumes of the Library of Congress—then housed in the Capitol—on August 24, 1814 did construction of the central rotunda and towering dome begin. The building was finally finished by the end of the Civil War when the current cast iron dome and

Freedom, the statue of capping the dome, were finally completed.

❖　　❖　　❖

Among the magnificent interior spaces in Washington is the **CAPITOL ROTUNDA**—183 feet high and almost 96 feet across. It is topped by Constantino Brumidi's epic fresco, *The Apotheosis of Washington.* The artwork shows the first president attended by allegorical figures, including those representing the original thirteen states. Brumidi, who had worked on the Vatican, died while working on the frieze that encircles the rotunda seventy-five feet above the floor. John Trumbull, a onetime aide to General Washington, executed four of the paintings at floor level where statues and busts, mostly of presidents, stand. More than twenty eminent individuals, including Pierre L'Enfant and presidents Lincoln and Kennedy, have lain in state in the Rotunda.

❖　　❖　　❖

Clio, the Muse of History, stands inside Carlo Franzoni's marble sculpture, *Car of History,* in the **CAPITOL'S STATUARY HALL.** She records events as they occur. It was once a whimsical Congressional tradition to set the clock as far backward as necessary to complete the day's business. Statuary Hall, which salutes notable former members, served as the House chamber until 1857. Portraits of former speakers of the House line the Speakers' Lobby. The original papers of President Andrew Jackson are among the artifacts on display in the Old Senate Chamber. Jackson served in both the House and Senate before leading American forces against the British in the Battle of New Orleans during the War of 1812.

On January 12, 1932, **HATTI OPHELIA WYATT CARAWAY**, a Democrat of Arizona became the first woman elected to the Senate.

❧ ❧ ❧

In 1999, the Senate held its second impeachment trial, that of **PRESIDENT WILLIAM CLINTON**.

❧ ❧ ❧

CONGRESS was installed in the completed north wing of the unfinished Capitol in 1800 after a ten-year residence in Philadelphia, during the construction of the national capital in Washington, D.C.

❧ ❧ ❧

On January 21, 1861, **SENATOR JEFFERSON DAVIS** of Mississippi gave his farewell address in the Senate before leaving to become president of the Confederacy.

❧ ❧ ❧

GPO, or the Government Printing office was established in 1861, and remains one of the largest printing plants in the world. Among the things it prints is *The Congressional Record and Federal Register.*

❧ ❧ ❧

On November 2, 1920, **WARREN G. HARDING** became the first incumbent senator to be elected to the office of the president of the United States.

❧ ❧ ❧

ANDREW JOHNSON became the first president to be impeached. His trial began in the Senate on March 30, 1868. It ended when the Senate acquitted Johnson by one vote. Seven years later Johnson became the first former president to serve as a senator.

❧   ❧   ❧

Founded in 1793, the **LIBRARY OF CONGRESS** is America's oldest national cultural institution and the world's largest universal collection of thought and creativity. It is housed in the three buildings: the grandiose Jefferson Building, a 1938 annex named for President John Adams, and a modern nine-story repository dedicated to President James Madison, built in the 1970s. In 1993, the LOC accepted its symbolic one hundred millionth acquisition, a collection of watercolors and pencil drawings.

❧   ❧   ❧

The Jefferson Building of the **LIBRARY OF CONGRESS** is named after President Thomas Jefferson who sold 6,487 works from his collection of from his library to Congress to restock Congress's "library apartment" at the Capitol after the meager collection was destroyed by the British in 1814. Many of the books were in French and others were, at the time, deemed "too philosophical" by members of Congress. Only congressional members and esteemed researchers are admitted to the building's Members' Room. The Great Hall, leading to the equally sumptuous Main Reading Room, accentuates the Library's reputation as a temple of knowledge.

❧   ❧   ❧

In 1917, **JEANNETTE RANKIN** became the first woman to serve in Congress, three years before the ratification of the nineteenth Amendment which gave women the right to vote.

On February 25, 1870, **HIRAM REVELS** of Mississippi became the first African-American senator to be sworn into office.

❖   ❖   ❖

On August 28-29, 1957, **SENATOR STROM THURMOND** of South Carolina filibustered against the 1957 Civil Rights Act. He spoke for a record 24 hours and 18 minutes, making it the longest speech in Senate history.

❖   ❖   ❖

Architect Cass Gilbert designed the **UNITED STATES SUPREME COURT BUILDING**, but only after Justice William Howard Taft, the only person to serve as both president and a High Court justice, persuaded Congress to construct a building to house the tribunal. Prior to 1935, the Court met at the Capitol and even in nearby taverns. On a pediment above the building's inscribed dedication to "Equal Justice Under the Law," allegorical icons to Liberty, Order, and Authority are joined by more modern figures. Beside the imposing stairway is James Earle Fraser's figure, *Contemplation of Justice.* The Court's proceedings in its sumptuous chambers are open to the public from the first Monday in October through late April.

❖   ❖   ❖

On July 1, 1845, **DAVID LEVY YULEE**, a Democrat from Florida, became the first Jewish senator to serve in the U.S. Senate.

❖   ❖   ❖

Monuments & Landmarks

A memorial amphitheater near the Tomb of the Unknowns in the center of **ARLINGTON NATIONAL CEMETERY** is the site of state funerals as well as annual Memorial Day and Veterans Day ceremonies. Every American president of the twentieth century has presided over such gatherings. Arlington National Cemetery is located in northern Virginia, directly across Memorial Bridge from the Lincoln Memorial, on land once owned by George Washington Parke Custis, the adoptive grandson of George Washington, and later by Custis's daughter, Mary, and her husband, Robert E. Lee. The estate was named in honor of the Custis family's ancestral home in Virginia's Tidewater region. The visitor center at Arlington National Cemetery contains historical displays about the cemetery and its history, as well as a small gift shop. Arlington National Cemetery has more than doubled in size since the U.S. Civil War. The first person interred was a Confederate soldier who had died in captivity. Many of the five thousand original gravesites were crude affairs, as at first only unidentified soldiers or those whose families were too poor to retrieve the remains of their loved ones were buried at Arlington—their gravesites noted with wooden markers. Today more than two hundred and fifty thousand veterans, including presidents Taft and Kennedy, prizefighter Joe Louis, and orator William Jennings Bryan—and some family members—lie in Arlington National Cemetery. Also entombed there are astronaut Virgil "Gus" Grissom and the remains of the seven Challenger crewmembers. Flags are permitted at gravesites only during the Memorial Day weekend.

THE ARMED FORCES MEDICAL MUSEUM, first opened in 1863, is a popular place to visit, especially by school-children who delight in the morbid. It was started during the Civil War to house specimens gathered from the battlefields—i.e. amputated limbs—to be studied to help doctors reduce loss of life and limbs in battle. Among the popular exhibits are a part of Lincoln's skull and the bullet-riddle neckbones of his assassin John Wilkes Booth.

BLAIR HOUSE on Lafayette Square is used to host visiting dignitaries. It was here at the beginning of the Civil War that Robert E. Lee was offered the command of the Union Army. In 1951, armed Puerto Rican terrorists broke in and unsuccessfully attempted to reach President Harry Truman, who was living there during a White House renovation.

THE BRITISH EMBASSY COMPLEX is the second largest diplomatic mission in Washington. Designed by Sir Edwin Landseer Lutyens, one of the greatest architects of his generation, it resembles a Queen Anne-style country house. Also on the grounds is a famous

statue of Winston Churchill giving the victory sign with his right hand, with his ever-present cigar in his left.

✣ ✣ ✣

THE BUREAU OF ENGRAVING AND PRINTING is a popular visitor attraction that cranks out billions of paper bills—and billions more postage stamps—each year.

✣ ✣ ✣

THE CONGRESSIONAL CEMETERY is the capital's oldest graveyard and is the resting place of photographer Matthew Brady, Vice President Elbridge Gerry—who devised "gerrymandering"—march king John Philip Sousa, and FBI Director J. Edgar Hoover.

✣ ✣ ✣

THE CRYSTAL CITY complex in Arlington along the Potomac River offers spectacular views of Reagan National Airport and monumental Washington. The U.S. Navy, giant defense contractor McDonnell Douglas Corporation, and an array of high-tech research and consulting firms are among the tenants in millions of square feet of office space here. The complex, which has won several national architecture and landscape awards, also includes an enclosed shopping mall, health clubs, several hotels, and more than thirty-two hundred condominiums and apartments. The Arlington Symphony Orchestra holds concerts in an amphitheater, and residents enjoy a 1.5-acre water park, sixteen smaller parks, extensive public art—including interior tapestries and murals—and a climate-controlled pedestrian concourse that connects to a shopping mall and Metro station.

✣ ✣ ✣

THE CUSTIS-LEE MANSION, or "Arlington House," overlooks the Arlington National Cemetery grounds. In 1861, with Robert E. Lee commanding Virginia's Confederate forces, the mansion was seized by federal troops. A two-hundred-ten-acre section of the surrounding estate was set aside as a military cemetery, some say out of hatred for Lee by Union Quartermaster General Montgomery Meigs who had lost a son in battle. Following the Civil War, the cemetery's superintendent lived and worked in Arlington House. In 1933 it was transferred to the National Park Service, which gradually refurbished the house. In 1955 the residence was designated a memorial to Robert E. Lee, and some original and many period furnishings have since been obtained to restore its antebellum flavor.

THE FBI BUILDING, which cost $126 million to build, opened in 1974, and was the most expensive project ever undertaken by the federal Public Buildings Service. The fortresslike structure was quickly lampooned by architectural critics—one called it the "Nightmare on Pennsylvania Avenue." Even FBI Director J. Edgar Hoover stuck a note in bureau files that read, "That's the goddamnedest ugliest building I've ever seen." But FBI Headquarters is a popular visitor attraction because of its engrossing tour, which covers everything from a stash of confiscated guns to a rogues' gallery of gangsters whose capture brought fame to Hoover and the bureau. Visitors get a peek, too, at the FBI crime laboratory that pioneered computerized fingerprinting, firearms matching, and suspect sketches, as well as DNA analysis.

THE FEDERAL TRIANGLE complex of behemoth buildings was modeled after the Louvre and constructed under the guidance of Treasury Secretary Andrew Mellon and the city's Fine Arts commissioners. It replaced a shantytown, but its army of bureaucrats who rushed from the buildings at workday's end drained the life out of Washington's old downtown. No one who found work building the Commerce, Justice, and other department headquarters complained, however, as it came in the throes of the Great Depression of the 1930s. Not just carpenters and masons got jobs; some of the nation's finest Depression artwork, created under the auspices of the Works Progress Administration, lines the halls of Triangle buildings.

❖   ❖   ❖

THE FOLGER SHAKESPEARE LIBRARY, built by industrialist Henry Clay Folger, has a collection of over a quarter million volumes that extends from the Renaissance through the eighteenth century in addition to its collection of 79 copies of Shakespeare's First Folio—of which there are only 240 known to exist. The library also sponsors the Folger Theatre Group, a resident acting company.

❖   ❖   ❖

After the assassination of President Abraham Lincoln at **FORD'S THEATER** in 1865, outrage ran so deep that its owner was forced to close down. The facility was converted into government offices where, in 1893, twenty-two clerks were killed when a floor collapsed. The building has held a Lincoln assassination exhibit since 1932, but only after restoration and reopening of the theater by the National Park Service in 1968 were a tour and carefully researched exhibit put in place.

The latter includes a careful re-creation of the president's box and a display of artifacts taken from Lincoln's body. Visitors also tour the Petersen House across the street where Lincoln died.

⚜   ⚜   ⚜

Georgetown University founded in 1789, is America's oldest Catholic university. Its hilltop tower can be seen for miles along the Potomac River.

⚜   ⚜   ⚜

George Washington University—once called "Columbian University—relocated to "Foggy Bottom," in 1912, west of the White House on Pennsylvania Avenue. It is a neighborhood of Federal-style row houses—many of which the university occupied.

⚜   ⚜   ⚜

The Hirshhorn Museum houses the Smithsonian Institution's modern art. Architect Gordon Bunshaft designed the 1974 drum-shaped granite-aggregate and concrete building that is elevated on four gigantic piers. The avant-garde museum, which traces the roots of modernism to the early eighteenth century, is named for Latvian-born Joseph H. Hirshhorn, whose 1966 bequest of twelve thousand works of modern art formed the bulk of the collection. The building of four stories and a balcony overlooking the Mall features an open inner core. The Hirshhorn's multi-terraced sculpture garden, with its own reflecting pool, lies several feet below the Mall. Each year, the Hirshhorn produces an eagerly anticipated film series.

THE HOLOCAUST MEMORIAL MUSEUM is a remarkable, sometimes disturbing, addition to the Washington museum scene in 1993. It is on Independence Avenue at the National Mall. Names and photographic portraits of victims of Nazi terror in Europe are some of the least graphic exhibits. Architect James Freed incorporated elements of concentration camps and gas chambers and other symbols of the persecution of millions of Jews, Gypsies, homosexuals, dissidents, and others. Each visitor receives an identity card of a victim of the same sex and approximate age, containing background on the person's life and death. The museum also makes its database available to Holocaust survivors and descendants to help them trace the fate of friends and relatives.

❖   ❖   ❖

HOUSE OF THE TEMPLE, SCOTTISH RITE was designed by John Russell Pope and completed for Washington's Masons in 1910, is modeled after the Mausoleum of Halicarnassus, one of the ancient world's Seven Wonders, in what is now Turkey.

❖   ❖   ❖

HOWARD UNIVERSITY, founded in 1867, initially trained preachers to serve freed slaves. The academically rigorous, primarily African-American university is named for Union General Oliver O. Howard, who directed the Freedman's Bureau. Howard's divinity school, designed by Charles Oakley, dates to 1870 when it was a Franciscan seminary.

❖   ❖   ❖

THE IWO JIMA MEMORIAL—properly, the Marine Corps War Memorial—completed by Felix de Weldon in

1954 is the world's largest bronze sculpture and is located at Arlington National Cemetery. It was inspired by Associated Press photographer Joe Rosenthal's image of five marines and one Navy corpsman raising the American flag atop Mount Suribachi during World War II.

❖ ❖ ❖

THE JEFFERSON MEMORIAL, designed by architect John Russell Pope, is inspired by the Roman Pantheon. The memorial was erected along the Potomac River Tidal Basin between 1938 and 1943. Because of wartime metal shortages, however, Rudolph Evans's bronze statue of Thomas Jefferson was not completed and installed until four years later. The statue is encircled by Ionic columns and four panels containing excerpts from Jefferson's notable writings including the 1776 Declaration of Independence.

❖ ❖ ❖

THE JOHN F. KENNEDY CENTER FOR THE PERFORMING ARTS designed by Edward Durrell Stone was built along the Potomac River on an old brewery site in 1971. Robert Berks's bust of President Kennedy in the Grand Foyer weighs three thousand pounds. The Kennedy Center is one of Washington's most popular attractions, usually drawing over 10,000 visitors a day.

❖ ❖ ❖

THE KOREAN WAR VETERANS MEMORIAL was not dedicated until 1995, four decades after the Korean War, a distant, sometimes forgotten, conflict. Much of the $18 million raised to build the memorial in a grove on the National Mall came from veterans themselves and from donations from Korean corporations operating

in the United States. The memorial's striking elements include Frank Gaylord's nineteen stainless-steel troopers patrolling through juniper bushes and granite rows that suggest Korea's tilled terrain; and Louis Nelson's polished granite wall-on which are etched the visages of thousands of support personnel, from pilots to M.A.S.H. medical corpsmen. "Freedom," reads one inscription at the memorial, "is not free."

❖   ❖   ❖

LAFAYETTE SQUARE across from the White House has been a traditional assembly ground for political protest. It honors the Marquis de Lafayette's triumphant return to the United States in 1824. Clark Mills's equestrian statue of Andrew Jackson dominates the park.

❖   ❖   ❖

THE LINCOLN MEMORIAL was completed in 1922. Dominating the Lincoln Memorial is Daniel Chester French's statue of the seated sixteenth president. It is made from twenty separate marble blocks that the sculptor seamlessly joined over thirteen years. Architect Henry Bacon's memorial that houses the statue is modeled after the Greek Parthenon. Its thirty-six Doric columns represent the states of the Union at the time of Lincoln's assassination in 1865; the names of the forty-eight states at the time of the memorial's completion are inscribed along the building's frieze. The texts of Lincoln's Gettysburg Address and Second Inaugural are carved into the memorial's marble walls.

❖   ❖   ❖

MOUNT VERNON, George Washington's Virginia homestead atop a Potomac River bluff—built in 1743 by his half-brother, Lawrence—recalls George's days as a gentleman farmer. Here, two hundred slaves helped the family harvest maize and wheat, raise dairy cows, and spin cotton and wool. When Washington died, he owned ninety thousand acres in Virginia and another forty thousand in what is now West Virginia. America's preservationist movement can be traced to the purchase and restoration of the Mount Vernon Estate, which had fallen into ruin, by the Mount Vernon Ladies' Association in 1860.

⚜   ⚜   ⚜

Ever since it opened during the 1976 U.S. Bicentennial, the Smithsonian's **NATIONAL AIR AND SPACE MUSEUM** has ranked at or near the top of Washington tourist destinations. It stretches three blocks long—685 feet long and 225 feet wide. Along with its displays of rocketry, space exploration, and futuristic travel, some of its most popular exhibits have been the oldest. They include the Wright Brothers' flyer flown in man's first controlled and sustained flight at Kitty Hawk, North Carolina, in 1903 and the Spirit of St. Louis, the craft that Charles Lindbergh's flew solo, nonstop across the Atlantic in 1927. Favorites, too, are IMAX theater presentations on a screen five stories high that challenge the imagination and the senses. Like other Smithsonian museums, Air and Space also has a renowned research library.

⚜   ⚜   ⚜

The original Corinthian columns removed from the U.S. Capitol during 1957 renovations form an imposing peristyle at the 446-acre **THE NATIONAL ARBORETUM**, the U.S.

Agriculture Department's research and education facility. The columns languished in a lot for a quarter century until landscape designer Russell Page hit upon the idea of creating an "acropolis" at the arboretum. With financing from benefactor Ethel Garrett and approval from Congress, Page created a portico of columns, reclaimed Capitol stones, and a water stair. The National Arboretum is home to the National Bonsai Garden and the nation's official collection of herbs. The latter, containing more than eight hundred varieties, is the world's largest. The arboretum's gardens also show off boxwoods, dogwoods, azaleas, and historic rose displays.

THE NATIONAL BUILDING MUSEUM—originally the Pension Building—is an elaborate 1877 structure designed by Army Quartermaster General Montgomery Meigs, which held the staff that oversaw the pension benefits to Civil War veterans. Outside, its astonishing, twelve-hundred-foot-long terra cotta frieze depicts aspects of Civil War military life. As the National Building Museum, this monolith houses imaginative architectural and urban-design exhibits. Its Great Hall is a favorite inaugural ball locale.

THE NATIONAL GALLERY OF ART consigns its modern-art collection to a fittingly stark East Wing. Andrew Mellon, benefactor of the original National Gallery in 1941, had purchased enough land for a later expansion. The 1978 East Building, whose trapezoidal footprint matches the unusual site where Pennsylvania Avenue, the National Mall, and Capitol Hill converge, was designed by Gold Medal architect I.M. Pei. It

often houses smash visiting exhibitions, modernist or not. In 1999, the National Gallery used still more of its reserved land for a new sculpture garden to display its modern-art statuary. Each winter, its fountain becomes a popular ice rink.

✤   ✤   ✤

In Washington, the stuffed African bush elephant—the largest ever recorded—inside the Smithsonian's 1910 **NATIONAL MUSEUM OF NATURAL HISTORY** has been a place where families and friends, dispersed among the Mall's many attractions, traditionally meet or rejoin each other. Dinosaur bones, gems, anthropological displays, and even an insect zoo are among the other exhibits. The National Museum of American History, opened in 1964, has its longtime-favorite exhibits including First Ladies' gowns and the original Star-Spangled Banner. It is also the repository of everyday American artifacts such as clocks, bicycles, washing machines, and even the Woolworth's lunch counter where a sit-in was organized in the 1960s.

✤   ✤   ✤

The Byzantine-style Basilica of the **NATIONAL SHRINE OF THE IMMACULATE CONCEPTION**, on the grounds of Catholic University, is the Western Hemisphere's largest—and world's eighth-most spacious—house of worship. Bishop Thomas J. Shahan, the university's rector, returned from Rome in 1913 with Pope Pius X's support for building a shrine to the Virgin Mary. Bishop Shahan described his vision as a "hymn in stone." Not until 1959 was the upper church, replete with marble and mosaics, completed and dedicated. The shrine can accommodate up to six thousand worshipers. Each of its sixty chapels and oratories repre-

sents a story from the history of the Catholic Church. The shrine's 329-foot Knights' Tower was a gift of the Knights of Columbus.

❖   ❖   ❖

THE NAVAL OBSERVATORY is the source and authority of time in this country, as well as providing astronomical data for navigation and legal purposes. The Observatory provides data on three types of time: Universal Time, based on the rotation of the earth; Ephemeris Time, determined by the obrit of the earth around the sun; and lastly Atomic Time, measured by a cesium beam atomic clock.

❖   ❖   ❖

THE OLD EXECUTIVE OFFICE BUILDING—originally the State, War and Navy Building—was built between 1871 and 1888 to hold the three cabinet departments. Designer Alfred Mullett later committed suicide in despair over the slow payment for his work. His French Second Empire-style creation was judged by Mark Twain as "the ugliest building in America."

❖   ❖   ❖

THE OLD POST OFFICE BUILDING, built in 1899 to house the main post office, was once described by the New York Times as "a cross between a cathedral and a cotton mill." It is a looming Romanesque-revival building along Pennsylvania Avenue and has survived many attempts to tear it down after the Post Office Department left in 1934. Those who venture up the open-air elevator to the 315-foot tower that holds its giant clock—each of whose hour hands measure seven feet long—get one of the best panoramic views of the capital city. Eventually tenants such as the National

Endowment for the Arts occupied upper floors, and the airy atrium was turned into a food court and indoor mall that is popular with bus groups.

❖ ❖ ❖

PERSHING PARK, in the middle of Pennsylvania Avenue, is astonishingly serene. Its greenery screens a dozen charms including a waterfall, a small skating rink, and a granite tableau recalling General "Black Jack" Pershing's exploits. Pershing and twenty-five thousand of his soldiers marched up the Avenue and under a temporary Arc de Triomphe at the close of World War I.

❖ ❖ ❖

THE PHILLIPS COLLECTION, near Dupont Circle and opened in 1921, is America's oldest museum of modern art. . Renoir's *Luncheon of the Boating Party* is one of its prized possessions.

❖ ❖ ❖

THE RENWICK GALLERY, a part of the Smithsonian Institution, was Washington's first sizable art museum. It was designed by James Renwick Jr. to hold the collection of William Corcoran. In 1897 Corcoran's holdings moved to larger quarters, and the building was transformed into a courthouse. Returned to Smithsonian ownership in 1966, it was named for Renwick and restored as a gallery of French Renaissance art.

❖ ❖ ❖

ROCK CREEK CEMETERY is the resting place of two U.S. Supreme Court justices and, where, in 1890, Henry Adams commissioned sculptor Augustus Saint-

Gaudens to create a monument to his dead wife. First Lady Eleanor Roosevelt often visited the statue, called *Grief,* which critic Alexander Wolcott deemed "the most beautiful thing ever fashioned by the hand of man on this continent."

❖   ❖   ❖

The arching stone bridges and 1,750 acres of woodlands of **ROCK CREEK PARK** stretch from Georgetown into Maryland. The area was spared from development when the federal government created one of the first national parks in 1890. There much earlier, at Fort Stevens, Confederate skirmishers had reached the capital city but were repulsed. Rock Creek Park is laced with twenty-nine miles of hiking paths and ten miles of equestrian trails, but automobile commuters often clog its winding roadway. The park features a nature center, amphitheater, golf course, tournament-quality tennis courts, and the National Zoo, which is a branch of the Smithsonian Institution. Washington's zoo was one of the nation's first to receive giant pandas from China.

❖   ❖   ❖

It was almost twenty years after the death of **FRANKLIN DELANO ROOSEVELT** before the nation's longest-serving president was remembered with a memorial—a humble block of Vermont marble on the National Archives Building lawn. Its simplicity respected Roosevelt's own wishes, expressed to Justice Felix Frankfurter in 1941, but public sentiment for a grander memorial eventually prevailed. In the mid-1990s, landscape architect Lawrence Halprin's tribute to F.D.R., complete with a waterfall and a "touching wall" for the visually impaired, rose in West Potomac Park. Inside four

open-air "rooms" are several statues, including those of Roosevelt himself, an Appalachian couple, a figure listening to a "fireside chat," and men in a bread line.

❖ ❖ ❖

St. John's Church has become known as "the Church of Presidents." Presidents James Madison, James Monroe, Martin Van Buren, William Henry Harrison, John Tyler, Zachary Taylor, Franklin A. Pierce, and Chester A. Arthur were among this Episcopalian church's parishioners. And the church bell has tolled with the death of each president who has died in office.

❖ ❖ ❖

The Smithsonian Institution began in 1849 in a Norman-style "castle" designed by James Renwick Jr., after whom the Smithsonian's Renwick Gallery of design and crafts is named. The Smithsonian owes its beginnings to James Smithson, a wealthy English scientist who never visited the United States. He left half a million dollars—a fortune in 1829—to found, specifically in Washington, "an Establishment for the increase and diffusion of knowledge of men." Renwick built Smithsonian Castle out of local sandstone. The building housed all facets of the operation—administration, laboratories, lecture halls, and art galleries. The Smithsonian secretary and his family even lived there. The Castle is now the information hub for visitors. Today the Smithsonian is an independent membership organization with multiple museums and galleries whose scholars conduct research and mount scientific expeditions around the world.

❖ ❖ ❖

UNION STATION built in 1903 was a Beaux Arts transportation palace designed by architect Daniel Burnham, major-domo of the 1893 Chicago World's Exposition. Lorado Taft's 1912 statue and fountain on Union Station's plaza honored Christopher Columbus. The terminal's grand presidential suite is now a fine dining room. The East Hall, which once held its own white-tablecloth restaurant, is now a chic shopping arcade. Union Station's West Hall was the ticketing and baggage-check alcove.

⚜   ⚜   ⚜

U.S. NAVY MEMORIAL, which was dedicated on October 13, 1987, features a lone bronze seaman who walks patrol atop a world map etched into a granite floor. Nearby is the U.S. Naval Heritage Center.

⚜   ⚜   ⚜

THE VIETNAM VETERANS MEMORIAL still collects dog tags, teddy bears, poems, flowers, and more. And visitors are still apt to see a loved one tracing a name from "the Wall." There are actually two polished granite walls, each 246.8 feet long, meeting at a 125-degree angle to form an open wedge. Maya Lin, a Yale University architecture student, designed the memorial and it was completed in 1982. Two statue groupings—including Glenna Goodacre's tribute to women who served as nurses in Southeast Asia—have since been added to the site in Constitution Gardens on the National Mall. Approximately fifty-eight thousand names are etched into "the Wall."

⚜   ⚜   ⚜

The Washington Monument rises just over 555 feet above the city and took thirty-six years to complete. Construction of the gigantic obelisk, containing an estimated thirty-six thousand marble stones—including 192 contributed by states, nineteenth century organizations, and foreign governments—began in 1848. But attention to the task, as well as funding, were diverted by the U.S. Civil War and its aftermath. Finally, on December 6, 1884, the monument was topped by a marble capstone and a—then rare and expensive—nine-inch pyramid of cast aluminum.

❖   ❖   ❖

The Washington National Cathedral, atop the city's highest point at Mount Saint Alban, soars higher than the Washington Monument. The architecture of this Protestant Episcopal cathedral—formally known as the Cathedral Church of Saint Peter and Saint Paul—was supervised by Philip Hubert Frohman for fifty-one years into 1971. The enormous cathedral, whose memorial, thanksgiving, and interfaith services have fulfilled Pierre L'Enfant's vision of a great "church for national purpose . . . equally open to all," was dedicated in 1907 by President Theodore Roosevelt, who exclaimed, "God speed the work!" No such thing happened, however. The Gothic cathedral remained in one stage of construction or another, down to the last gargoyle, for the next eighty-three years.

❖   ❖   ❖

Some of Washington's most prominent citizens keep apartments at the **Watergate**. The building, just up the Potomac River from the John F. Kennedy Center for the Performing Arts, will long be synonymous in American history with the 1972 break-in of

Democratic National Committee Headquarters that led to President Richard Nixon's resignation two years later. The burglars kept the Watergate in view from a much less pricey hotel across the street.

❖   ❖   ❖

For a century it seemed everyone who was anyone stayed at the **WILLARD HOTEL**—the "Hotel of Presidents"—on Pennsylvania Avenue. Julia Ward Howe wrote the words to "The Battle Hymn of the Republic" there. Ulysses S. Grant greeted supplicants in the lobby, which inspired the term "lobbying." Calvin Coolidge resided there during his entire vice presidency. But the Willard turned shabby after World War II and was closed for demolition in 1969. Saved after a remarkable preservationist campaign, it and its splendid, concierge desk, dining room, and "Peacock Alley" hallway were restored.

❖   ❖   ❖

THE WOODROW WILSON HOUSE was a surprise present by the former president to his second wife, Edith Bolling Wilson, who had assumed many chief executive's duties as "secret president" after Wilson suffered a stroke during his second term. Following a Scottish tradition, Wilson presented his wife with a key and piece of sod from what would become a magnificent garden. After the president's death in 1924, Mrs. Wilson continued to live in the house until her own death in 1961. She bequeathed the house to the National Trust for Historic Preservation, which maintains it as "a unique time capsule of Washington history in the 1920s."

Legends and Lore

Near the White House on Constitution Avenue was where the Potomac River used to reach in the 1820s. **PRESIDENT JOHN QUINCY ADAMS** used to take morning swims here. A female reporter, Anne Royall, who had been refused interviews with the president, reportedly took his clothes and refused to give them back unless the president allowed an interview.

❖   ❖   ❖

THE BALTIMORE SUN BUILDING is considered to by some to be the country's oldest surviving skyscraper. Over a hundred years old, it was designed by Alfred B. Mullett who also designed the Old Executive Office Building.

❖   ❖   ❖

BRADDOCK'S ROCK is a large rock formation that used to be near the Potomac River. Legend has it that the English General Braddock landed here on his way to his death during the French and Indian War. A young George Washington was then under Braddock's command.

❖   ❖   ❖

FRANCES HOGDSON BURNETT, the famed English author of *Little Lord Fauntleroy*, lived and wrote most of her famous

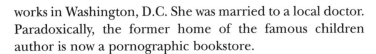

works in Washington, D.C. She was married to a local doctor. Paradoxically, the former home of the famous children author is now a pornographic bookstore.

❧   ❧   ❧

AARON BURR, who killed Alexander Hamilton in a duel in 1804, was vice-president to Thomas Jefferson at the time. Although under indictment for murder, he served out his term. But while in office, he also unsuccessfully planned to seize the Western territory of the United States along the Mississippi. He was tried for treason but was acquitted on a technicality. After a time in Europe, he returned to a law practice in New York.

❧   ❧   ❧

CHERRY TREES are a famous image in Washington. The Japanese government in the early part of the twentieth century made a gift of 3,000 white Yoshino cherry trees, and they were planted around the Tidal Basin. By the end of the century only 125 of the original trees had survived, but new trees were planted as the original trees died.

❧   ❧   ❧

Dueling was for a time a problem in the capital. The practice was finally outlawed after **CONGRESSMAN JONATHAN CILLEY** of Maine was killed in a duel by Representative William J. Graves of Kentucky on February 24, 1830. The duel was fought on account of political remarks by Cilley which Graves found offensive. Anti-dueling legislation was helped through Congress by former President Andrew Jackson—himself no stranger to dueling.

❧   ❧   ❧

CHARLES DICKENS, the famous English novelist, lived for a time in Washington in 1842. However, his opinion of the city was

not a fond one. He wrote: "It is sometimes called the City of Magnificent Distances, but it might with greater propriety be termed the City of Magnificent Intentions . . . Spacious avenues, that begin in nothing, and lead nowhere."

⚜ ⚜ ⚜

FOGGY BOTTOM was originally the nickname of the part of Washington known as Hamburgh. Some believe the name derived from the smokes and fumes of the gas plant, brewery, and glass factory that were once located there. Others believe it referred to the fog that came of the nearby Potomac River.

⚜ ⚜ ⚜

Legend has the origin of the famous drink, the **GIN RICKEY**, as created by one Colonel Joseph Rickey, a lobbyist and bartender in Shoomaker's Tavern, one of the renowned bars that made up Washington's "Rum Row." It was originally a "Whiskey Rickey" made of whiskey, Apollinaris water, and lime juice. Gin later became the alcoholic ingredient.

⚜ ⚜ ⚜

THE GEORGETOWN PHARMACY, run by Doc Palinsky for forty-eight years, was renowned as a gathering place for Washington's elite. Franklin Delano Roosevelt stopped by for ice cream and cigarettes. In a later period, the pharmacy became the site of an "11-year free brunch," which played host to such notables as newsman David Brinkley, columnist Art Buchwald, and novelist Herman Wouk.

⚜ ⚜ ⚜

CHARLES GUITEAU, who assassinated President James Garfield was hanged on June 30, 1882 at the "Washington Bastille," the Washington Jail. According to witnesses Guiteau was so drunk as he was led up the scaffold that he was cheerful, and

chattering and singing, "I'm so glad I'm going to the Lordy . . ." as guards held him steady for his final moments.

❧   ❧   ❧

EDWARD EVERETT HALLE wrote "Man without a Country" at the Tabard Inn in 1863. The story was for a time one of the country's most popular stories. It was the tale of Philip Nolan, a fictional naval officer who goes into exile after being involved with Aaron Burr's treason. Nolan expresses the wish never to hear or read of the United States, which he does for fifty-five years.

❧   ❧   ❧

In 1893, inventor **CHARLES FRANCIS JENKINS** built the first movie projector in Washington that was demonstrated three years later in New York City. He also established the first television station in America on Connecticut Avenue NW in Washington. It was built in 1928 with the call letters W3XK. However, it was only able to transmit images of dark silhouettes.

❧   ❧   ❧

FRANCIS SCOTT KEY, a prominent lawyer who wrote "The Star-Spangled Banner," lived in Washington. In 1814, he happened to witness the English attack on Fort McHenry in nearby Baltimore where the fort's commander defiantly flew the fort's flag amidst savage bombardment. Key's words were set to music, but did not become the national anthem until 1931.

❧   ❧   ❧

In 1859, near the present site of the Treasury building, **PHILIP BARTON KEY**, son of Francis Scott Key—the author of the "Star-Spangled Banner—was shot and killed by Daniel E. Sickles, a congressman from New York. Key was having an

affair with Sickles's wife. Sickles however was acquitted of murder on the grounds of temporary insanity, the first time that defense was used successfully.

❖   ❖   ❖

SINCLAIR LEWIS lived in Washington while completing his most famous novel, *Main Street*, from 1919 to 1920. He was hoping to sell 10,000 copies, but within a year the novel sold 180,000.

❖   ❖   ❖

Washington, D.C. is one of the few cities to have an official **LOVER'S LANE**, which runs between Massachusetts Avenue and R Street NW. The lane received its name in 1900, where its reputation as a favorite place for assignations was already well-established.

❖   ❖   ❖

In the nineteenth century, **MURDER BAY**, located on Constitution Avenue, was the city's most squalid and dangerous slum. As one police official described it, "Here, crime, filth and poverty seem to vie with each other in a career of degradation and death." During the Civil War, the area was nicknamed "Hooker's Division," when Union General Joseph Hooker ordered that the city's prostitutes be concentrated in the area. The city's brothels remained centered in the area until the building of the Federal Triangle began in the 1920s.

❖   ❖   ❖

THE OCTAGON HOUSE has an interesting history. Although it only has six sides, it has eight angles, thus its name. After the burning of the White House in 1814 by the British, President Madison and his wife lived here for a time. But the house is infamous for its more spectral visitors. The ghosts of Colonel

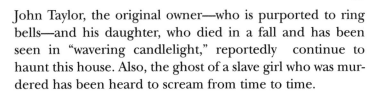

John Taylor, the original owner—who is purported to ring bells—and his daughter, who died in a fall and has been seen in "wavering candlelight," reportedly continue to haunt this house. Also, the ghost of a slave girl who was murdered has been heard to scream from time to time.

❖ ❖ ❖

The last blacksmith shop in Washington, D.C. operated by **G. Herbert Ofenstein**, closed on January 30, 1959. The owner reportedly worked there for fifty-six years, and was known for the feat of shodding 225 horses in one day.

❖ ❖ ❖

Ryder's Castle during the mid-nineteenth century was home to a group called the "resurrectionists—body snatchers— who would rob newly filled graves. Under the leadership of a woman named Maude Brown, they would steal bodies and sell them to out-of-town medical schools. It was a major problem that the police were unable to stop until the mid 1890s.

❖ ❖ ❖

John Philip Sousa, the "March King," was born in Washington, DC on November 6, 1854. He joined the U.S. Marine Band at the age of thirteen and was its bandmaster from 1880 to 1892. His famous compositions include "Stars and Stripes Forever" and "The Washington Post March."

❖ ❖ ❖

The Surratt House, located in China Town, was a boarding house during the Civil War. It was described as the "nest where the egg of treason was hatched" and the site figured in the assassination of Abraham Lincoln. Mary Surratt, who ran the house, was hanged as a co-conspirator.

❖ ❖ ❖

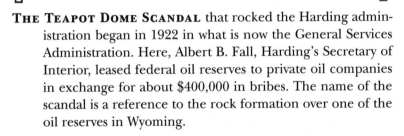

THE TEAPOT DOME SCANDAL that rocked the Harding administration began in 1922 in what is now the General Services Administration. Here, Albert B. Fall, Harding's Secretary of Interior, leased federal oil reserves to private oil companies in exchange for about $400,000 in bribes. The name of the scandal is a reference to the rock formation over one of the oil reserves in Wyoming.

❧ ❧ ❧

THOMPSON'S RESTAURANT, which long discriminated against African Americans, in 1953 became the target of a Supreme Court decision that forced the city to provide equal access for everyone. It was the beginning of the breaking down of the barrier of segregation paving the way for the gains of the Civil Rights movement in the 1960s.

❧ ❧ ❧

THE WASHINGTON HILTON was the site of the assassination attempt on Ronald Reagan by John Hinckley on March 30, 1981. Reagan as well as James Brady, his press secretary, and F.B.I. agent Raymond Martin were wounded in the attack.

❧ ❧ ❧

During the Cuban Missile Crisis of 1962, the **YENCHING PALACE**, a Chinese Restaurant, played an important role in successfully averting war. In secret, two men, an ABC newsman representing JFK and Alexander Fomin of the Soviet embassy, representing Krushchev, worked out the terms that ended the crisis.

❧ ❧ ❧

The city's most spectacular fire took place in January 1928 at the former site of the Dulin and Martin China store. The fire was fought by the entire Washington, D.C. fire department as well as almost thirty companies from neighboring

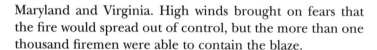

Maryland and Virginia. High winds brought on fears that the fire would spread out of control, but the more than one thousand firemen were able to contain the blaze.

❧ ❧ ❧

The conditions of the streets in Washington have always been a source of complaints. One nineteenth-century observer wrote: "The avenues, as they are pompously called . . . are the worst roads I passed in the country. . . . Deep ruts, rocks and stumps of trees every minute impede your progress and threaten your limbs with dislocation." Today there are still innumerable complaints about the potholes.

❧ ❧ ❧

The streets of Washington were originally letters of the alphabet, but there never was a "J" street. Local legend had it that it was an insult to Chief Justice John Jay. But the explanation is much simpler: the I and J of the lettering used for the street signs looked almost identical in the nineteenth century, thus there as no J street. And I street is often written as "Eye" so no to be confused with 1st street.

❧ ❧ ❧

On December 31, 1916, Washington was the site of a horrible trainwreck. Two trains collided at Terra Cotta station. The larger of the two trains slamming into the smaller, stationary train filled with passengers at 61 mph. Reports indicated that the impact was like an "explosive shell." Blood seemed to cover everything. In all, forty-six people died and seventy-nine were injured.

❧ ❧ ❧

Washington is the site of one of the few gas stations to be considered a landmark. Located at 22nd and P streets NW. Built in the 1930s, it has arched windows and classical columns. It still functions today as a Mobil station.